BOOKS BY ROD McKUEN

stanyan street & other sorrows

stanyan
street
&
other
sorrows

ROD McKUEN

RANDOM HOUSE NEW YORK

C O N T E N T S

FOREWORD

I sing more Rod McKuen songs than songs
by anybody else.

In the beginning they were those little gems
that I sandwiched in between the razzle-dazzle
material that got attention. Now they get
more requests and more attention than any
of the other songs I perform. I finally had
to record a full album of his material including
some of the poems in this book.
I admire Rod's work, that must be evident.
More unusual, in a words and music world
where alliances are easily broken and
friendships are taken lightly, we have remained
close friends from the day we were
introduced by Neely Plumb. Our only rivalry
being who records Rod's songs first.
Me or him.

I can't imagine performing a concert without
including *Stanyan Street*, and I can't imagine
ever again being without this little book.
For me they are not merely poems,
they are an extension of a man who is able
to put into words what so many of us
feel and cannot say.

GLENN YARBROUGH

AUTOBIOGRAPHY

For my mother

1.

I remember hearing children
in the street outside
above the noise
of pots and pans and bickering.
They had their world
I had my room.
I envied them only
for the day long sunshine
of their lives
and their fathers.
Mine I never knew.

2.

I grew
not necessarily erect.
I bent sometimes
but never to the lowest branch
and learned to love the smell
of people's bodies making love to me
as much as I loved lilacs.

3.

I try to play as many games
as games there are.
To lie a little's not so bad
if it gets you through the night.
Bach and The Supremes help too
and I've a cat
who's learned to like my music.

4.

I read sometimes obituaries
in towns that I pass through
hoping I might find a man
who spells his name the same as me.
If he's dead then I'll know where he lived
and if he lived.

5.

In the end
the songs I sing
are of my own invention.
They mirror what has happened to me
since I was abandoned by my father
and by love.

6.

I stay alone
confined to me
imposing my philosophy on no one else
(The words that make this book
were written for myself
except a few that were a letter
written to a love now gone
who lived on *Stanyan Street.*)
but I have saved them up
and give them here
to those I hope might understand.

May 16, 1966

STANYAN STREET

for Glenn and Ellen
Jocelyn and Tony
Flo and Eddie
and . . .

I.

You lie bent up in embryo sleep
below the painting of the blue fisherman
                    without a pillow.
The checkered cover kicked and tangled on the floor
the old house creaking now
a car going by
the wind
a fire engine up the hill.

I've disentangled myself from you
                    moved silently,
groping in the dark for cigarettes,
and now three cigarettes later
                    still elated
                              still afraid
I sit across the room watching you—
the light from the street lamp coming through the
    shutters
hysterical patterns flash on the wall sometimes
                    when a car goes by
otherwise there is no change.
Not in the way you lie curled up.
Not in the sounds that never come from you.
Not in the discontent I feel.

You've filled completely
this first November day
with Sausalito and sign language
                 canoe and coffee
                        ice cream and your wide eyes.
And now unable to sleep
because the day is finally going home
because your sleep has locked me out
I watch you and wonder at you.

I know your face by touch when it's dark
I know the profile of your sleeping face
the sound of you sleeping.

Sometimes I think you were all sound
kicking free of covers
and adjusting shutters
moving about in the bathroom
              taking twenty minutes of our precious time.

I know the hills
      and gullys of your body
           the curves
                the turns.

I have total recall of you
and Stanyan Street
because I know it will be important later.

It's quiet now.
Only the clock
moving toward rejection tomorrow
breaks the stillness.

2.

I have come as far away
as means and mind will take me
trying to forget you.
I have traveled, toured
turned a hundred times in the road
hoping to see you rushing after me.

At night,
though half a world away,
I still hear you sigh in several sizes.
The breathing softer when you're satisfied.
The plip-plop body machinery back to normal.
Remembering how warm you are
and how defenseless in your sleep
never fails to make me cry.
I cannot bear the thought of you
in someone else's arms
yet imagining you alone is sad.

And in the day
my mind still rides the bridge
from Sausalito home.
I do not think
me and San Francisco
will be friends again
we share too many troubles.
Stanyan Street and other sorrows.

3.

We try so hard to make each other frown
I sometimes wonder
if we haven't been together much too long.
The words that work the wonders are so few
that they seem foolish anymore.

Is this a kind of loving too,
a chocolate bar that tastes good at the time
but kills the dinner later on?
Could be our appetite will go
till even memory's not a feast.

But there are times
when you can smile in such a way
that I'd forget a ten year war
and lie down in your shadows' shadow
and live on sounds your stomach makes.
In these brief times
I could die against your side
and never make a warning sound
content to suffocate
within the circle of your back.

5.

Three years
      (or maybe four)
have moved beneath the San Francisco wreckers
and their yard-long hammers.
Their caterpillar treads that transform brick
to dust-red powder.
Those giant cranes
that slice a roof down
with a single swing.

Some have never known the wreckers' rattle.
Those houses on Pacific that march toward posterity
restored by dilitantes from Jackson Square
painted up like aging actresses
with eye-shadow windows and rouge-red doors.
Some have had collections taken up
petitions passed from hand to hand.
Their widows walks scraped free of dirt
and green grass planted where the weeds once grew.

These houses almost shiny new
that crowd Nob Hill
   and march down Lombard in a row
were saved to show the glory of the past.

There was a house on Stanyan Street
that took a single day to wreck
and that includes an hour spent
at tin-pail lunch on sandwiches and beer.

They carted off the lumber and sold it by the pound.
The bricks at least, ten cents a piece,
now make a Marin garden wall.

But there is little salvage to be had
in bent and broken nails
and things that might have been
if I'd had wiser eyes
or been a fisherman
                    in blue.

OTHER SORROWS

for Skip and Neely
Katie and Hale
John and Pamela
and Peter

HOLIDAYS

Holidays were made for lonely people.
I always meet the best of these
when holidays are near.
Rented rooms become the place to go,
$\qquad\qquad\qquad$ not fireworks
or carnivals
$\qquad$ or musical parades,
but rented rooms with granite basins
and people who forget your name
before you finish going down the stairs.

Holidays mean the most
when you're celebrating
what you've found yourself.

Love is a season
and holidays like signposts
mark the time.

APARTMENT 4E

The girl upstairs
is entertaining again,
I could set my clock
by the footfall on the stairs.

I see her sometimes,
coming and going on the stairs
or going to the market.

Sometimes I hear her late at night
playing sad music
or walking overhead.
She smiles in the daytime,
but not at me.

CHANNING WAY, I

It's always the strangers that do the most damage.
The ones you never get to know.
        Seen in passing cars
                mirrored in windows
and remembered.

              And the others—
the ones who promise everything, then go away.

Sometimes I think people were meant to be strangers.
Not to get to know one another,
not to get close enough to damage the heart
made older by each new encounter.

But then,
someone comes along
and changes all that.
For a while anyway.

Still, as the years go by
it's easier to remember
the streets where it happened
              than the names
and who was the one on Channing Way.

BROWNSTONE

Birds and butterflies
dart
       down
               canyons
between tall buildings
looking for a place to hide
as the sky above the city darkens
and the rain begins
            timid at first—unsure
then creeping onto window ledges
and foraging along the sidewalk.

They're tearing down the building across the street
and the old woman who sat cushion high
behind the flower boxes
                              is gone.
Even the children who played along the broken side-
    walk
                         have disappeared
and their hop-scotch lines are washed away.

Only the multi-colored cat
preening in the shop window
is unconcerned
as night begins.

DO NOT TELL ME YOUR NAME

Do not tell me your name
why you came to town
what you like to do on Sunday
your favorite poet
                movie
                comic strip
your age and next of kin in case of accident.

Say instead that I am warm
let your touch talk
let the motion in the darkness speak
then go away if you must
but not while I'm looking.

MOTH

Awakening
this morning
after the first night of being loved
I heard a disillusioned moth
flapping at the window glass
trying to reach the morning sunlight.
And the sun,
long fingers of it,
came through the window
picking out the dust in special corners.

In the pre-dawn hours
             lying together
all arms and legs and breathing
with the rain not so far away
and morning coming too soon
I hoped never to see the sun again.
             And now
your face and the sun
have made this room
with only ceiling sky
and avenues of sunlit dust
beautiful.

SPRING SONG

Don't hurry spring
the wind still trembles
in the empty trees
and dead geraniums stand still
in Spanish Harlem window boxes.
Another week perhaps
when skaters leave the pond.

Now for a while longer
we can have the park to ourselves.

I need a while more with you just now,
there are some things
I don't yet know.
Do you like the color blue
       do I worry you when I frown
where were you
when I was growing up and needed somebody?

FOR S. C.

I do not know
what is more beautiful
than your tangled black hair
on a white pillow.
I have thought about it all afternoon
and decided not even butterflies or children
or the blossoms in the hills above the beach
can compare.

If I had money
I would not buy a comb or a red ribbon
to decorate it.

Instead I might charter worlds
so you could walk in them
and everyone could see your hair.

CAMERA

I stand *just so*.
Your camera winks me into permanence
acne scars
        tired eyes
wrinkles on my forehead
more naked than I have ever been
      (especially to one
      I love so very much).

I used to be afraid to look completely real
the sun was just my friend sometimes
when brown from sea and sky made things all right—
always afraid to be anything but young
and envying beauty
      even on the face of strangers.

Is this what growing up means
the reality of lighting over public mirrors?
Or is my confidence in love so great
that I worry not
to let you see me at my worst?

JIMJANN

I wanted you
that day at the beach
because you were beautiful
and because you smiled
and because I knew your world
was different.

But I lost you
even before we had met
and I ran on the beach all day
to relieve the tension.

Better to live
in a birdless country without sun
than go your way alone—always.
But what could I have said?
Your smile was a warm wall.

POEM

The smell goes first.
The smell that closed rooms have
when women are about.

No coffee smell,
no sweet stale smell of bath,
no hair smell on the pillow,
no smell of beds too long unchanged.

I kept the window closed all day
trying to retain what little of you there was left.

And now the darkness like firecrackers ringing in my
    ears,
trying to sleep in the same unchanged bed
calling back old images
to make the evening come out right.

CHILD

They fall from your hips quietly
starting down around your thighs, then gone.
You step out of them
and become a naked little girl.
Then into bed
and for a long moment nothing happens
then the sigh starts it
the legs let go.

Girls have little hollows in their backs
and hold the whole of autumn in their arms
their smiles are warm valley smiles.

When you sit
or stand
or talk
or walk
or look around
or smile
you look like a little girl
but you feel like a woman.

CHANNING WAY, 2

I should have told you
that love is more
      than being warm in bed.
                        More
than individuals seeking an accomplice.
Even more than wanting to share.

I could have said
that love at best is giving what you need to get.

But it was raining
and we had no place to go
and riding through the streets in a cab
                    I remembered
that words are only necessary after love has gone.

BENGIE

I was wrong to invade your little world
of museums and kites and pigeons flying.
                I have deceived you.
Not by meeting other peoples' eyes
or knowing arms that were not yours
but by pretending to be young at heart
and invading your stuffed-animal world.

I should have stood aside when your kite
                    came
           sailing
      down
but I had to run and help.

DAY SONG / NIGHT SONG, I

I.

The freckled morning
               moving into day now,
I stand at the window half dressed,
watching the snow melt as quickly as it falls.

A hundred blank windows
in the building now going up across the street
look back at me.
My expression is as empty as theirs,
as the long slow business
of learning how to live alone begins again.

2.

The shadowed afternoon
                moving into night now,
I close the door behind me
and hurry down the stairs.

You know
Saturday night is better than Friday.
If you don't make out
you can take home
the great American consolation prize,
thirty cents worth of love,
              the Sunday paper.

I'LL TRY
TO SHOW YOU
SPAIN

for Jacques Brel
Emmett Bright
and Jack Kearney

SOME THOUGHTS FOR
BENSON GREEN ON HIS
TWENTY-SEVENTH BIRTHDAY

Having just gone through the year myself
I know that twenty-seven can be hard.
But there are Sunday breakfasts
                      and April fields
and blue on blue
                      and green growing things
to change all that.
I know that spring is hard because you wait for
   summer
and fall is hardest of them all—
            because you must not be alone when win-
            ter comes.
I know
that love is worth the time it takes to find.
Think of that
   when all the world seems made of walk-up rooms
and hands in empty pockets.

I know your smile
and it is much too warm to waste on people in the
   street

               (though smiles are plentiful)

and
I know
that if you keep the empty heart alive a little longer
love will come.

             It always does,
maybe just at the last moment, but it will come

                    you must believe that
or else there isn't any reason to be twenty-seven.

ORLY FIELD

For Doug Davis

I often
wonder why you ran so fast,
if it was all to end at Orly Field that day.

You might have stopped in Spain awhile
and let the sun go singing in your head.
Or walked the hills in Hydra.
Or even stayed at home.
Atlanta's not that bad in summertime.

You might have listened for the wind
and got to know it better.
They say it comes in handy later on.
I might have been a better friend
if I hadn't trusted time.

If the dead can hear the living
raise your head a little
and I'll try to show you Spain.

LOS ANGELES
6/5/65

FOR P.B.

I do not know
if you smiled when you were dying
or cursed your friends
for the little attention we paid you of late
or how you spent your last full hour alive.
I do know that I was saddened when I heard the news.

Mostly
because you gave yourself to me once
without invention or restraint,
for that I still remember you
and love you.

NEW YORK
5/12/60

RICHARD FARINA

For Mimi

He died as though
he'd read his own book
and believed that folks should die that way.

They shouldn't you know.
Especially the poetic few
who say so much for all of us
with knotted tongues.

These men should die in poppy fields
old and withered, used up, done,
their last days spent as children once again.

Twenty-nine is young enough to dig a well
and sow at least a dozen kids
and leave another song or so for us to sing
and hike a half dozen hills.
Poets after all should walk
and be content to take their time.

But when you straddle a machine
to race along the sea
you should be prepared to die
when the machine dies under you.

I hope he was.

SAUSALITO
5/11/66

COMFORT

If we could do it all again
    motor bike through roman cities
in the rain
    watch the cats chase lizards in the forum
    and drink bad wine from mouth to mouth
I probably would try
to love you harder than I did
I probably would smile a smile
much better than the ones you knew
for I was just rehearsing then
imagining what easily might happen
in years to come

it is not just you I love
    (or even Roman rain)
or all the times you rattled on my window
after twelve o'clock.

I love the smell of rooms—
where you have been
the foreign touch of things I never knew
until you came along.

I even love your enemies
because they drive you to my arms
for comfort.

MONTEREY 10/11/53

The leave over
the last bus loading
I take the seat by the window
weary already of the journey back to camp.

The war went well today
there was a ship sunk in Pusan Harbor
and a bridge on the Whan River sabotaged.
They say by Christmas it will all be over.

The news reached me
as I lay in bed this morning
listening to Madame Butterfly on the radio
and wishing I had a more interesting home
to come back to than Oakland.
I mean there is only the lake here
and I am growing too old for that
so—after the war what?

Back at camp
the bronze bellied men of war
lie upon their narrow cots
and search the ceiling
oblivious to the wall of night.
Tomorrow on a California beachhead
we will be assured by a drill instructor
that there are real battles to fight.

DOG PEOPLE, SEATTLE

rain . . . and the middle of the month
brings them all out

The line assembly men
who rivet at Boeing
and keep their secret well
the sad-eyed beautiful ones
who stay at home all week
reading Elliot and Keats
even the depraved old ones . . . perennial.
The girls with colored glasses for eyes.
Me
a soldier on weekend pass
neither strong of muscle or of will
neither young to be here
nor old to stay away.

Undiscovered and alone
till someone says . . . *hello.*

TOKYO HARBOR,
FIRST IMPRESSION

Riding through the cities on the train
I saw dirty people at dirty windows
and bare children walking railroad ties
chalking messages on sidewalks.
Sometimes there were bicycles waiting at crossings
and oxcarts carrying who knows what
and fat mamasans resting in the shade
eating rich lunches.

At the noon hour
we threw them candy bars
and cigarettes
and felt happy and foolish about it.

Children waved
Gave us the finger
and got candy bars in return.

I can't help thinking that we Americans
leave behind a universal sign language
in lands we occupy or conquer
a phallic finger raised to all
these people think it means hello
Good God
what are alphabets for?

SECOND IMPRESSION

Way around the lake
beyond the trees that crowd the moat
there is a warm place I remember
where all the high garret rooms have skylights.
Mamasan is in command
and for a fee
she'll forget anything.
You can get there in a 70 yen cab.

Listen if the night will let you
to songs I sing and things I say
tomorrow when the air is different
you'll forget and go away.

STATE BEACH

He turned
and moved to go into the water
she followed close behind.
The sun caught the color of her hair
and the bronze of his legs
and I caught them both
held them in my gaze
till they were out of sight
splashing in the sun
lost in the waves.

I think I have never been in love more than now
here on a native beach
watching other lovers
do familiar things and make familiar love.
I think I have never missed you more.

And as the last October sun
goes beyond the ocean to its resting place
and the umbrellas are folded
the rumpled pants and rumpled dresses
slipped over the wet bathing suits,
the sound of a Tokyo spring
echoes in my ears
I walk with you down dark streets
and the rain comes down like tears.

SOME POEMS
FOR MY ANIMALS
&
KEARNY STREET

for Katie
Batman
& Sloopy

SOME THOUGHTS ON FINDING MY CAR
BROKEN INTO ONE SUNDAY MORNING
AROUND THE CORNER FROM
THE HUNGRY I

How well I sang my songs that night
the audience was quiet to a man
I felt some kinship with all people
until I went into the dark
and found that like Enrico says
it is a jungle after all
and there are animals of prey
we've not yet named.

Whoever slit the belly
of that wild young mustang
and hoped to find a treasure
got instead a meager haul.

They took the things I value most
my toothbrush and a razor
some poems and a song
I'd stuffed up in a suitcase
together with a list of names
I'd been ten years collecting—
no good to anyone but me.

What a fire it will make
that antique address book
those names that have no faces
and now I'll judge my popularity
by those who ring *me* up.

What pawn shop of the mind
can index all those numbers
new people in the last four days
are all the ones that I remember.

Enrico says the worst thing is
that some black stranger
poured among my things
and has a knowledge of
my secret self.

Insurance covers underwear
suits and shaving kits
the latest Catherine Sauvage disc
but who's to put a premium
on notebooks full of foolish things
a pasted joke an anecdote
a lyric started not yet sung.

That address book thick and black
I'd like to have it back
for it contains old and worn
a laundry list of love.

THE YELLOW UNICORN

This morning I woke up just in time to see
                                    a yellow unicorn
eating the low branches from the linden tree outside—
then into the green he ran
and was gone.

Alone now—again
with sunlight the color of the unicorn
moving over the wall
                                and low clouds
and the hot July of New York about me,
I think about Diamante's green eyes
or maybe the one called Dov
or others . . .
                (I cannot forget
                the images of some lone persons
                who look at me and maybe for a while
                                        seem to want me
                they wear love in their eyes
                the way a child wears new
                on his first day at school.)

I have loved some
whose arms and names I never knew
the girl in Peter's bar
                a face on the train
mostly in the last year
I've felt this kind of love.

And one night
hearing a big woman say
                as she was stroking my head
I wish there had been someone like you when I was
    young
                        I went away
and began to love strangers
people I would see only once
on buses and in bars or walking by themselves
                in quiet places.
And in this last year there must have been a hundred
who never knew
a funny little boy watched *them* and loved
                                them.

POEM

I have no special bed.
I give myself to those who offer love.
Can it be wrong?
Lonely rivers going to the sea
                    give themselves
to many brooks in passing.

So it is with me
undiscovered and alone
till someone says the magic word.

You'll see me then
some weekend waiting
and if you do
            say hello.

KEARNY STREET

The house on Kearny Street
where I came and went on weekends
                              is the same.
The hill above is summer green
the sky a foggy blue
and children still march by each day at three o'clock
foraging back from school.
The hill and Kearny Street are still the same
                              but I have changed.

No more the winning smile
the hasty song
the happy stare of love
the young heart leaping in the dark room.
And no more the wild young man
who talked too quickly and too loud
of love he owned and wished to give away.

Seldom the sun
catches me lying in bed late any more.
Seldom the pigeons gargling in the grass
see my form stretched out upon the lawn.

I pace unfamiliar streets now
attempting new solutions to old problems
and the answers seldom come.

But there was a time
in the fall and winter of the year
when the sun's bright yellow mingled with the fog
and Kearny Street in San Francisco was the whole
   world.

Sometimes I'm sorry for love once known
it doesn't justify the years you spend remembering.
I was always timid about your loving me anyway
knowing the eagle doesn't hunt flies
and that worlds were larger than our love.
But I am happy still
that even for a moment
you laughed in my direction
and chased my nakedness down a lonely beach.
For maybe six months of love
is worth the lifetime you spend looking,
and marmalade
            and oysters for breakfast one morning
and knowing you tried to love me
                    is enough.

For love is only moments here and there
it comes and goes quietly I think.
You hear it like silver bells
tied about the throats of cats
            (now near — now sounding far away.)

I was loved on Kearny Street.
But no more the young heart leaping in the dark
    room.

THOUGHTS ON CAPITAL PUNISHMENT

There ought to be capital punishment for cars
that run over rabbits and drive into dogs
and commit the unspeakable, unpardonable crime
of killing a kitty cat still in his prime.

Purgatory, at the very least
                    should await the driver
    driving over a beast.

Those hurrying headlights coming out of the dark
that scatter the scampering squirrels in the park
should await the best jury that one might compose
of fatherless chipmunks and husbandless does.

And then found guilty, after too fair a trial
should be caged in a cage with a hyena's smile
or maybe an elephant with an elephant gun
should shoot out his eyes when the verdict is done.

There ought to be something, something that's fair
to avenge Mrs. Badger as she waits in her lair
for her husband who lies with his guts spilling out
cause he didn't know what automobiles are about.

Hell on the highway, at the very least
                    should await the driver
    driving over a beast.

Who kills a man kills a bit of himself
But a cat too is an extension of God.

EIGHT SONGS

for Dave Hubert

ELLEN'S EYES

If I'd not known Ellen's eyes
perhaps the day would be
easier to understand
gentler to me.

If I hadn't memorized
the sounds she makes
while close to me
I might have filled my memory up
with August skies or July sea.

But as it is my memory world
has little room for skies,
all the space is taken up
remembering Ellen's eyes.

BEFORE THE MONKEYS CAME

We'll go wild into the noon
to find what love there is to find
an angel on the bedpost
or a demon in the mind
and we'll be happy as we were
before the monkeys came
and put the flowers into pots
and gave love sinful names.

When apple trees were apple trees
and not the curse of man
and all the mountains piled high
were only heaps of sand
there were no *yellow* roses then
the roses all were red
and lovers slept on grassy banks
and never knew a bed.

We'll go wild into the noon
and try to be the same
the way we were awhile ago
before the monkeys came
when every street was Eden street
and Man our only name
that was oh so long ago
before the monkeys came.

THE VOYEUR

While walking in a lonely wood
I saw a big man fall a tree
his muscles bulging in the sun
he never said hello to me.

Once in a gray-green meadowland
I saw a girl with yellow hair
she didn't pause to speak my name
or even know that I was there.

Some children playing in the street
and bouncing balls against the wall
went right on playing in the street
and never noticed me at all.

I've been a stranger all my life
to everything and everyone
just passing through this lonely world
until my journeying is done.

I'M STRONG BUT I LIKE ROSES

Once in every lifetime
a little bird may come
alone and forgotten
knocked down by the sun.
Every man may choose
to turn and walk away
or take the bird into his hand
and bid him stay.

A man may like roses
and still be big and strong
and what is life without
a little bird's song?

I'm strong but I like roses
and if a bird should come
I'll keep him
till his singin's all done.

I'm strong but I like roses
and when he has to fly
I'll pick another rose
and watch the days
go slowly by.

CHASIN' THE SUN

Kin went to London on a love scholarship
all of us wished him a marvelous trip.
If he thought he had troubles before,
look at him now he's got two dozen more.
One of those bright young men
runnin' out after the fun.
One of those bright young men chasin' the sun.

Eddie moved out of his coldwater flat
and into a penthouse. Can you picture that?
If he thought he had sorrows before
look at him now he's got two dozen more.
One of those bright young men
runnin' out after the fun.
One of those bright young men chasin' the sun.

Owen gave up his job sellin' shoes
his bills were picked up by a lady named Crews.
If he thought he had worries before
look at him now he's got ten thousand more.
One of those bright young men
runnin' out after the fun.
One of those bright young men chasin' the sun.

All of those bright young men
runnin' out after the sun.
All of those bright young men
how pale they all look in the light of the sun.

THE SUMMERTIME OF DAYS

In the summertime of days
a man is nothing more
than a tear in some old year
that was cast aside by God.

In the summertime of days
we are as we must be
shadows all on our way to fall
if not eternity.

And if we must look for heaven
then heaven must surely be
in arms that are warm
and smiles if they tender be.

In the summertime of days
I'll ask for nothing more
than a face and a quiet place
that was cast aside by God.

ALL OF ME IS MINE

If I'm still alone by now it's by design
I only own myself, but all of me is mine.
But it's hard sometimes when strangers
offer you a dime.
I only own myself, but all of me is mine.

If I still drink water when some folks drink wine
I only own myself, but all of me is mine.
But it's hard when city windows dance
with candleshine.
I only own myself, but all of me is mine.

The price you pay for sunshine
can sometimes be quite dear
when all you have to sell is youth
it's hard to lose another year
my only forced submission
has been the rape of time.
I only own myself, but all of me is mine.

THE LONELY THINGS

The silent rain that falls, the meadowlark
the winter wind that calls the lovers from the park
the sad and bitter song December sings
these are the lonely things.

The sun behind the clouds, the starless night
when you're alone in crowds the need for sudden
    flight
the empty loneliness that parting brings
these are the lonely things.

A taste of love too soon gone wrong
the sad mistaken heart that heard the sirens song
                    and sang along.

The waves that drum the shore at morning light
the friends that come no more to try and make things
    right
the hopes that fly too soon as though on wings
these are the lonely things.

ABOUT THE AUTHOR

ROD McKUEN was born in Oakland, California, at the end of the Depression. He grew up in California, Nevada, Washington and Oregon, and worked as a laborer, stunt man, radio disc jockey and newspaper columnist before serving in the army in Japan and Korea as a psychological-warfare script writer and member of the Korean Civil Assistance Command.

Returning home he was encouraged by his friend Phyllis Diller to perform at San Francisco's Purple Onion. During the engagement he was brought to Hollywood and put under contract to Universal-International as an actor. In 1959 he moved to New York to compose and conduct the music for Albert Mc-Cleery's highly lauded television series, *The CBS Workshop*.

He has played the major cabarets and concert halls of the world, and has written more than 900 songs. His material has been performed by Andy Williams, Danny Kaye, Elsa Lanchester, Eddy Arnold, Henry Mancini, The Kingston Trio and Glenn Yarbrough, among others. He spends seven months of the year in a house in the Hollywood hills, with a menagerie of cats and dogs, where he writes, records for RCA Victor, and runs a growing publishing and recording firm. The balance of his time he devotes to traveling and performing in Europe. This is his first volume of poetry. He is currently working on a novel. His new book of poems, *Listen to the Warm*, will be published by Random House in September, 1967.